SONGS AND STORIES FROM UGANDA

SONGS AND STORIES FROM UGANDA

By W. Moses Serwadda

Transcribed and edited by Hewitt Pantaleoni

Illustrated by Leo and Diane Dillon

Thomas Y. Crowell Company, New York

Designed by Meri Shardin

Manufactured in the United States of America

ISBN 0-690-75240-7
0-690-75241-5(LB)

Library of Congress Cataloging in Publication Data

Serwadda, W. Moses.
  Songs and Stories from Uganda.

  SUMMARY: Thirteen songs with accompanying stories
retold from Ugandan folklore.
  1. Tales, Ugandan. [1. Folklore—Uganda.
2. Folk songs, Ugandan] I. Dillon, Leo, illus.
II. Dillon, Diane, illus. III. Title.
PZ8.1.S4577So   398.2′09676′1   72-7556
ISBN 0-690-75240-7
ISBN 0-690-75241-5 (lib. bdg.)
          1 2 3 4 5 6 7 8 9 10

Contents

A Note from the Author   vi

Editor's Preface   vii

How to Pronounce Words in Luganda   ix

SONGS AND STORIES

  1   *'Keenene*   1

  2   *Nnoonya Mwana Wange*   7

  3   *Kaleeba*   11

  4   *Wavvuuvuumira*   17

  5   *Tweriire*   21

  6   *Nnyonyi*   27

  7   *Purrrrr Ce!*   33

  8   *Awo!*   41

  9   *Nsangi*   45

10   *Akanyonyi*   53

11   *Ttimba*   61

12   *Woowooto*   71

13   *Ca, Ca, Ca*   77

A Note from the Author

For a long time I have had a desire to see that Americans and Europeans understand our music and learn to sing it or play it. I know it will be an adventure for them, since they live in a different environment and have a different background.

Children all over the world have many things in common: they all want to learn about new things, things from other lands—birds, animals, snakes, trees, and beauties. Most of the songs in this small book will be about these things.

In my childhood, I found myself in an environment where music was a very common way of expression and relaxation. My grandfather was a chief in the Bukunja area on the northwest shore of Lake Victoria, so he had his own group of musicians in his enclosure. They used to play on various occasions such as succession ceremonies and other feasts. My father himself used to play fiddles and bowl lyres.

My grandmother was a very good storyteller. We grandchildren used to sit in the evenings around the fire in her house and listen to her stories and songs. We were always expected not only to be good, active listeners, but also to be able gradually to tell stories. Thus I came to know a lot of stories and the songs which often accompanied such stories.

Although I wrote this small book for children of school age, it has been written with care so that it can be useful to those who are studying African history and culture as well as African music. I know there is a lot that can be learned about Africa through its songs.

Munno ddala*

Moses Serwadda

Department of Music, Dance and Drama
Makerere University
Kampala, Uganda

* Yours sincerely

vi

Editor's Preface

Here are thirteen beautiful songs from the Baganda, a people of southern Uganda, a country in East Africa, northwest of Lake Victoria. Some of the songs go with stories, some with games or dances, and some are just to sing. They are authentic and traditional songs, well known and well loved. Some of the stories can be heard in other parts of Africa as well.

The tunes and rhythms are easy, but the language may seem strange to you at first. Take courage: just pronounce it about the way you would in English (there are some special helps to pronunciation on page ix).

Please *don't* sing these African songs in English. It sounds awful, and the African text is really not very hard, just different. Use the English translation to help you understand what you are singing, for it follows the meaning rather closely. Read it aloud when others need to know what you are singing about. You will find that the rhythm of the English and the rhythm of the song itself are very close, and this helps everyone remember the sense of what you are singing when you turn to the African words.

An African story is really neither read nor recited in Africa; instead, it is re-created on the spot at the time of the telling. The storyteller works upon the feelings and imagination of his audience. He mimes and dances; he sings the solo parts and his listeners respond by singing the choruses; he acts the various roles with a dramatic use of tone and inflection. What he does, and when he does it, are almost more important than the exact words he uses. We hope you will use these stories as a basis for a dramatic performance or storytelling session. When you do, remember you can vary or re-create the text yourself, as the African storyteller does.

Moses Serwadda, who lives in Uganda, supplied all the material, translated all the texts into English, and supervised their progress into final form. The editor accommodated the stories to the Western practice of reading alone, or aloud to others, and accepts full responsibility for the literary style of the result. When the African audience is quite familiar with certain details, or when a particular point is made visually rather than verbally, the African version of a story is apt to be so brief that the unfamiliar listener or reader would not understand it at all. In these cases the editor has tried to provide the missing parts.

The musical transcription of these songs is that of the editor, though here again Mr. Serwadda exercised keen supervision. Key signatures are justified by the clear tonic feeling of the songs, and by the fact that the musical staff used in the Western World represents the pitches sung by Mr. Serwadda without distortion.

A final word about rhythm. There are no heavy beats in this music. Use the bar line only as you would a place marker, not as an invitation to emphasize the next note. Try for a gentle flow rather than a punchy rhythm.

With thanks we acknowledge the help of Mr. M. B. Nsimbi, former Senior Education Officer in charge of Luganda language for the government of Uganda; of Mr. G. Kakoma, a Commissioner of Culture for the government of Uganda and formerly Inspector of Schools in music; and of Miss Anne Pellowski of the Information Center on Children's Cultures in New York City.

Hewitt Pantaleoni

Department of Music
State University College
Oneonta, New York

How to Pronounce Words in Luganda*

1. Vowels have just one sound, even when they are doubled:
   A has the sound of "a" in "father."
   E has the sound of "e" in "hey!"
   I has the sound of "i" in the name "Toni."
   O has the sound of "o" in "oak."
   U has the sound of "u" in "through."

2. If there are two vowels together, elide them, giving the second one the more attention.

3. Some consonants need special notice:
   C and KK and KY all have the sound of "ch" in "church."
   G is nearly always hard (but may be soft before "i").
   R is the sound of the middle letters of "fodder" when we say the word lightly and quickly.
   Ḷ has the sound of R above (but L is like ours).

4. Doubled consonants last longer than single ones.

---

* One of the peoples in southern Uganda is called the Baganda, and their language is called Luganda.

SONGS AND STORIES FROM UGANDA

1. 'Keenene

A village of the Baganda is not a cluster of houses in a circle or a square, but a series of small farms strung out along a road. The road runs above the forested valley, at the feet of the surrounding hills, for the Baganda do not live down in the forest. Their drinking water, however, comes from wells which are usually found there. The village well is therefore usually some distance away from the village itself.

"'Keenene" and "'keenu" are the way young children say the word for raspberry, "nkeenene."

ONCE UPON A TIME there lived a man and his wife who loved each other very much and were quite happy, except that they did not have any children. After they had grown quite old they had a boy and a girl, who grew up to be very obedient and helpful around the house.

Every day the children would go into the forest to gather firewood and to fetch water. The firewood they carried in their arms, or on their backs. The water they carried in clay pots on their heads.

Now it happened one day that the children could not find the two small pots they usually took to fetch water in. So they took two which were much, much larger. They went to the well and filled them up, but *unnhh!*, when they tried to lift them onto their heads, they just couldn't do it. They couldn't even drag them along the ground.

So they sat down under a big tree that grew by the well. The village seemed very far away. "How can we ever move these pots?" they sobbed. "Who will help us?"

Just then, what do you suppose? From behind the tree a large animal suddenly stepped out and said in a deep voice, "I will help you."

It did not growl, or glare, or show its teeth. Indeed, it was most friendly. It introduced itself as Baluba, and said it lived in the roots of a great tree in the forest not too far away. At first the children were scared nearly to death, but after a while they let Baluba put the heavy pots up onto their heads and thanked him politely.

"You are pleasant children, and well-mannered," said Baluba. "You must come to my house tomorrow and have a feast with me."

The children thought this was a fine idea. They thanked Baluba again, and went home.

The next day they came to the feast. There was plenty of food—roast corn, meat wrapped in banana leaves and boiled, peanuts and oranges, and milk to drink. For dessert Baluba gave them raspberries, as many raspberries as they could stuff inside themselves.

"Can we take some back to our father and mother?" they asked. So Baluba took a banana leaf and made up a large bundle of raspberries for them. Then he showed them the path which led back to their village.

As they walked along, they met with some people from their village, who were out looking for them. The people called out:

Mu - va wa?
Where've you been?

But when the children tried to answer them, the villagers kept inter-
rupting because they could see the berries through the folds of the
banana leaf:

SOLO: 'Kee - nu, 'kee - nu CH.: 'Kee - ne - ne!
Ber - ries, ber - ries . . . Rasp - ber - ries!

Off they all went to the village, the children swinging the bundle of raspberries and everybody singing.

Their parents were very glad to see them coming, and called out:

Mu - va wa?
Where've you been?

And the children, glad to be home again, swung the bundle of berries and sang with their friends the song they had made up together.

And that is what I saw.

2. Nnoonya Mwana Wange

This is a game for at least seven or eight players. One person is chosen as "parent" and another as "child." Form a circle, with plenty of room between players and several players between the "parent" and the "child."

Standing in place, the "parent" begins the song at the speed of a jog. When the chorus answers, the "parent" begins to chase the "child," both of them stepping in time to the music.

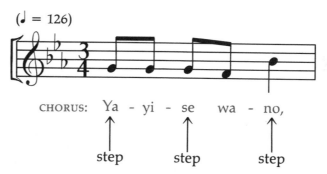

The "child" must weave in or out through every gap in the circle and not miss a one, and the "parent" must go exactly where the "child" has gone. While the "child" can jog silently, the "parent" must sing his part while moving.

The chorus holds hands to form archways, or they may clap to mark the steps of the chase. As the song gets faster and faster, neither "parent" nor "child" may jostle or hang on to a member of the chorus.

The game is over when the "child" is caught, or when the "parent" gives up. A new pair is then chosen.

Don't forget that "nnoo-" rhymes with "know."

Claps: ! ! ! ! ! ! (etc.)

PARENT: Nnoo - nya mwa - na wa - nge, nnoo - nya mwa - na wa - nge!
Look - ing for my dar - ling, look - ing for my dar - ling!

(The chase begins)

CHORUS: Ya - yi - se wa - no, ya - yi - se wa - no nga⌒a - ge - nda.
He just went by here, he just went by here on his way.
(She) (she) (her)

(A little faster)

PARENT: Nnoo - nya mwa - na wa - nge, nnoo - nya mwa - na wa - nge!

CH.: Ya - yi - se wa - no, ya - yi - se wa - no nga⌒a - ge - nda.

8

(Yet faster)

PARENT: Nnoo - nya mwa - na wa - nge, nnoo - nya mwa - na wa - nge!

CH.: Ya - yi - se wa - no, ya - yi - se wa - no ngaᴒa - ge - nda.

(And faster)

PARENT: Nnoo - nya mwa - na wa - nge, nnoo - nya mwa - na wa - nge!

*PARENT (coming in ahead of time): ngaᴒa - ge - nda.

CH.: Ya - yi - se wa - no, ya - yi - se wa - no ngaᴒa - ge - nda.

*Use this variation for the "parent" any time as a way of beginning the solo "Nnoonya mwana wange."

9

3. Kaleeba

IT HAPPENED ONE DAY that a bird with a beautiful voice settled on the branch of a tall tree growing near the well of a certain village.

A woman was filling her pot at the well. When it was full she put it on her head and started back to her house. As she passed by the tree, the bird started to sing:

(♩ = 108)

SOLO: Sse - mu - ka - zi◡a - ge - nda CHORUS: Ka - lee - ba! SOLO: Nɲa - mbi - ra◡a - ba - lie - ka◡e-
O wo - man pass - ing by, Look here now! Take a mes - sage home for

yo CH.: Ka - lee - ba! SOLO: *'Ki - nyo - nyi ki - ri ku lu - zzi CH.: Ka - lee - ba!
me. Look here now! Say a bird is here at the well Look here now!

SOLO: Kya - mba - dde◡e - nsi - mbi CH.: Ka - lee - ba! SOLO: E - nsi - mbi n'o - bu - tii -
Wear - ing cow - rie shells, Look here now! Cow - ries and ma - ny fine

*In this song pronounce both "ki" and "ky" as if they were "chee."

11

ti! CH.: Ka - lee - ba! SOLO: Kyo, kyo - kyi! CH.: Ka - lee - ba!
beads! Look here now! Look here now!

SOLO: Kyu - ka n'o - ndee - ba! CH.: Ka - lee - ba!
Turn back, look at me! Look here now!

What a beautiful song! she thought. Forgetting the pot of water on top of her head, she looked up to see the singer. *Crash!* The pot broke upon the ground.

My, she was angry! She scolded the bird, and tried to see where it was. She threw stones into the branches. She threw pieces of her broken pot.

The bird remained very still in its hiding place.

No one believed her story at home, and that made her madder than ever. People thought she was just making up excuses.

The bird played its little game all day long. Sometimes it would change the tune a little to make it even more lovely.

($\quad$ = 108)

SOLO: Mu - ka - zi ggwe⌢a - ge - nda CHORUS: Ka - lee - ba! SOLO: Nŋa - mbi - ra⌢a - ba - li⌢e - ka⌢e-
Wo - man that's pass - ing by, Look here now! Take a mes - sage home for

Many women lost their water pots.

Toward the end of the day a young girl came to the well. For her the bird made its song quite fancy:

(♩ = 108)

SOLO: Mu - wa - la ggwe◡a-ge -nda CHORUS: Ka - lee - ba! SOLO: Nŋa-mbi-ra◡a-ba - li◡e-ka◡e
Lit - tle girl pass -ing by Take a mes-sage home for

CH.: Ka - lee - ba! CH.: Ka - lee - ba!
yo n -ti◡e - ki-nyo-nyi ki - ri ku lu - zzi n - ti
me. You just say a bird is here at the well and he's

CH.: Ka - lee - ba!
kya - mba-dde◡e-nsi - mbi n - ti e - nsi - mbi n'o -bu - tii -
wear -ing cow - rie shells, He's got cow - ries and ma -ny fine

ti! CH.: Ka -lee - ba! SOLO: Kyo, kyo, -kyi! CH.: Ka -lee - ba! SOLO: Kyu - ka n'o -ndee -
beads! Turn back, look at

ba! CH.: Ka - lee - ba! SOLO: Kyo, kyo - kyi! CH.: Ka - lee - ba! SOLO: Kyu - ka n'o - ndee-
me!   Turn back, look   at

ba!   CH.: Ka - lee - ba!
me!

Crash!

Now it happened that some women of the neighborhood were visiting in the house of this young girl when she returned without the water. They listened to her story, and each of them told how she had lost her own pot in the same way.

Soon everyone in the village knew about the bird. They went to the well, and the men gathered around the tree to drive it away. No one could see it, so they shouted and threw stones, but the bird was careful not to make a move.

The men held council. Nothing could be done, they decided, but cut the tree down. They went and got their axes, and began to chop. *Po! Po! Po!*

Each blow made the branch tremble on which the bird was sitting, but still it did not move.

Finally, as the great tree fell crashing to the ground, the bird gave up its perch and flew away. From that day to this it has never returned.

And that is what I saw.

15

4. Wavvuuvuumira

In Buganda, that part of Uganda where the Baganda live, there is a certain large, reddish-brown bug that has a fondness for bamboo groves. When it flies one sees the inner wings, which are yellow and black like the body of our own bumble bee. If you say the name of this bug, "vvuuvuumira," with lots of "v," you will hear something of the sound it makes.

The Baganda treat animals as individuals in their stories by putting the syllable "wa" in front of their names. A dog—"mbwa"—becomes Dog when he is called "wambwa; a "vvuuvuumira" becomes Bamboo Bug when he is called "wavvuuvuumira."

This song is often sung as the second half of the lulling song "Ca, Ca, Ca" (No. 13 in this collection). The soloist simply starts at letter [A], page 18, when the last chorus of "Ca, Ca, Ca" has been sung, being careful to keep the music moving along.

($\textbf{.}$ = 76)

SOLO: Wa - vvuu - vuu - mi - ra   CHORUS: Le - kaↃo - mu - li - roↃo-
Mis - ter Bam - boo Bug   Please leave the hearth, let

mwa - na ye - ba - ke. SOLO: Vvuu - vuu, vvuu - vuu CH.: Le - kaↃo - mu - li - roↃo-
ba - by go to sleep.   Please leave the hearth, let

mwa - na ye - ba - ke. SOLO: Wa - vvuu - vuu - mi - ra CH.: Le-
ba - by go to sleep.   Mis - ter Bam - boo Bug   Please

kaↃo - mu - li - roↃo - mwa - na ye - ba - ke. SOLO: Vvuu - vuu - vuu,
leave the hearth, let ba - by go to sleep.

vvuu - vuu - vuu CH.: Le - kaↃo - mu - li - roↃo - mwa - na ye - ba - ke.
Please leave the hearth, let ba - by go to sleep.

SOLO: Wa - vvuu - vuu - mi - ra CH.: Ka - ti◡o - ko - la - ki◡o - mwa - na ye - ba - se.
Mis - ter Bam - boo Bug What are you do - ing? Ba - by's gone to sleep.

SOLO: Vvuu - vuu - vuu - vuu - vuu CH.: Ka - ti◡o - ko - la - ki◡o - mwa - na ye - ba - se.
What are you do - ing? Ba - by's gone to sleep.

(Growing softer)

SOLO: Wa - vvuu - vuu - mi - ra CH.: Ka - ti◡o - ko - la - ki◡o - mwa - na ye - ba - se.
Mis - ter Bam - boo Bug What are you do - ing? Ba - by's gone to sleep.

SOLO: Vvuu - vuu - vuu, vvuu - vuu CH.: Ka - ti◡o - ko - la - ki◡o - mwa - na ye - ba - se.
What are you do - ing? Ba - by's gone to sleep.

* "ki" is pronounced "chi" in this song.

5. Tweriire

The Baganda are a nation of independent farmers with small planta-
tions. For export they grow coffee, tea, sugar, tobacco, and cotton. For
themselves they grow millet and plantains. Millet is a grain which
grows like wheat. Plantains are like green bananas, but do not taste
as sweet.

ONCE UPON A TIME there lived a man who owned a large field of
millet. At the time of this story there was a terrible drought
and food was scarce everywhere, so the man and his wife grew their
crop very carefully.

But they were not the only ones who felt hunger that year. Great
flocks of birds came every day to attack the field and eat the grain.
The man, his wife, and their large family of boys and girls spent most
of their time shooing the birds away.

Now it happened one day that the man left with friends to hunt
water buffalo. His wife had to go take care of the family plantain
plantation. So the children were left to mind the field of millet all by
themselves.

At noon the man returned with buffalo meat for his family. His wife
returned from the plantation and started to prepare the midday meal.
The children, however, did not come in from the field of millet when
she called to them.

Annoyed and worried, she went to see what was the matter. *Oh!* There in the middle of the field were the children, dancing away, and all around them were the birds, singing and eating up the millet. When the children tried to shoo them away, waving their arms and crying "Swi! Swi!", it didn't seem to disturb the birds at all. They just ate and sang, and sang and ate, and kept the children dancing.

"What is going on here?" said the wife.

"Mother," said her children, "what a wonderful song the birds sing! When we came early this morning, they were already here, and we tried to shoo them away, really we did, and they hopped around a bit, but they would not fly away, and then they began to sing, and then we began to dance, we just had to, and now we are dancing and they are singing and you must join us! What a wonderful song!"

The wife scolded the children for letting the birds fool them like that. Then she ran about the field waving her arms to shoo them away herself. They hopped about a bit, but not one of them flew off. Instead, they began to sing their song again.

They sang so beautifully that soon the wife was standing still, listening. Then she began to dance to the rhythm, she just had to, and her children joined her. And so they went about the field, dancing and trying to shoo the birds away at the same time.

(♩ = 112)

SOLO: Tu - lee - ke tu - lye CH.: Twe - rii - re SOLO: Tu - lee - ke tu - lye,
Please leave us a - lone, Let us eat. Please leave us a - lone,

CH.: Twe - rii - re o - bu - lo - bwai - tu, twe - rii - re. SOLO: (Swi! Swi!)
Let us eat our mil - let, please, let 'us eat. (Nnh! Nnh!*)

CH.: Twe - rii - re SOLO: (Swi! Swi!) CH.: Twe - rii - re o - bu - lo - bwai - tu,
Let us eat. (Nnh! Nnh!) Let us eat our mil - let, please,

twe - rii - re SOLO: Tu - lee - ke, tu - lee - ke CH.: Twe - rii - re SOLO: Tu -
let us eat. Please leave us, oh leave us, Let us eat. Please

lee - ke CH.: Twe - rii - re o - bu - lo - bwai - tu, twe - rii - re SOLO: Tu -
leave us, Let us eat our mil - let, please, let us eat. Please

* A loud sound through the nose. You can make up other shoo-away noises, if you
want, and use them here.

23

lee - ke tu - lye CH.:Twe - rii - re SOLO: Tu - lee - ke tu - lye CH.:Twe - rii - re o - bu-
leave us alone, Let us eat. Please leave us a - lone, Let us eat our

lo - bwai - tu, twe - rii - re. SOLO: (Swi! Swi!) CH.: Twe - rii - re
mil - let, please, let us eat. (Nnh! Nnh!) Let us eat.

SOLO:(Swi! Swi!)CH.:Twe - rii - re o - bu - lo - bwai - tu, twe - rii - re.
(Nnh! Nnh!) Let us eat our mil - let, please, let us eat.

Now the husband was still at home, waiting for his lunch. Time
went by, and he grew more and more angry. Finally he went himself
to the field of millet to scold them all.

Well! There they were, dancing about in the middle of the field, and
the birds all around them eating up his millet! With a shout he dashed
into the field waving his arms, and started chasing the birds away.

Not a single bird flew off. Instead, they began to sing even more beautifully than before. They sang and sang, and finally the husband himself began to dance, even as he tried to scare them away.

For the rest of the day the family danced for the birds in the field of millet. No matter what kind of a noise they made to scare them away, the birds would not go, but kept on eating and singing.

When darkness came at last, they flew off, and the family went home for supper—happy, tired, and very hungry.

And that is what I saw.

6. Nnyonyi

A vigorous action song in jig time requiring no particular formation (though follow-the-leader is fun). The simplest action is to bounce from the ball of one foot to the ball of the other, in time to the music. Keep your legs flexed.

SOLO: Nnyo - nyi   CHORUS: te - ri - ma   mu - we - mba.
A   bird   does - n't   grow   sor - ghum.

Since the song is about birds, you can add some wing motions with your arms.

SOLO: Nnyo – nyi CH.: te – ri – ma mu – we – mba
A bird does – n't grow sor – ghum.

For a more vigorous variation, alternate a bouncing step on the right foot with a hopping step on the left foot.

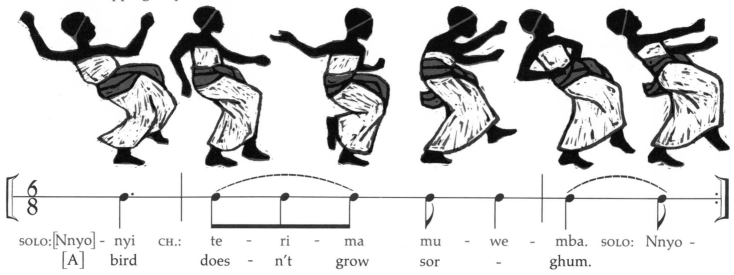

SOLO:[Nnyo]– nyi CH.: te – ri – ma mu – we – mba. SOLO: Nnyo –
[A] bird does – n't grow sor – ghum.

There are no musical cues for changing from one kind of motion to another. Simply do what you wish, or follow the leader (anyone can lead, and the leadership can change during the song).

The chorus sings the different verses in this song, not the solo leader. Therefore it is best to stick to just the first verse when playing this game outside, so that everyone can be together in the singing, although scattered about the play area. The solo leader should let his phrase "Nnyonyi" carry over into the sound of the chorus which follows.

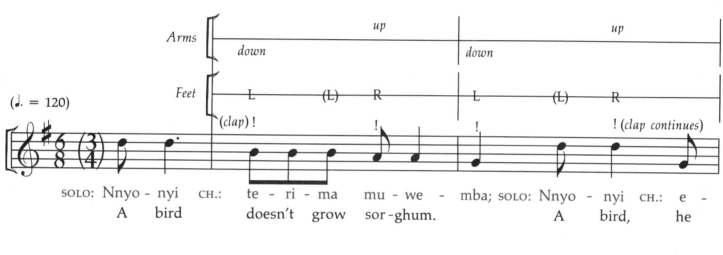

Nnyo - nyi!

sa - nga ma - li - mi - re. SOLO: Nnyo - nyi CH.: te - ri - ma kka - la -
finds them read - y to hand. A bird does - n't grow pep - per

Nnyo - nyi!

li. SOLO: Nnyo - nyi CH.: e - sa - nga mu - li - mi - re.
pods. A bird, he finds them read - y to hand.

7. Purrrrr Ce!

Let your audience get to know the story all the way through before you ask them to take the chorus part in the tale. Remember "c" has the sound of "ch."

ONCE UPON A TIME, in a village next to a forest, there lived a hunter and his wife.

He was a good hunter. His traps in the forest were placed so well and set so cleverly that not a day went by without his catching something.

His wife was a fine cook. She turned everything he brought her into a delicious meal. But there came a day when he could bring her nothing at all, for all of his traps were empty.

That day he was sad walking home through the forest. Then he heard something move, *purrrrrrrrrrr!* Looking up, he saw a tiny bird land on the branch of a nearby tree, *ce!* Quickly he picked up a stone, threw it at the bird, and killed it.

When he handed it to his wife to cook, she was careful to say nothing about its size. It was, she knew, the only thing he could find.

So she plucked the feathers off the bird. Then she cleaned out the insides and salted the meat thoroughly. Next she put a pot of water on the fire. While that was heating up, she went out to pluck several fresh leaves from the banana trees which she and her husband had planted behind the house.

She folded one leaf around the bird and another around some plantains (plantains look like large bananas but do not taste as sweet). Her pot was now boiling, so in went the bird and the plantains, and on top of them some more banana leaves.

When all was ready she placed some fruit and other food in front of her husband, and with it the bird still wrapped in its banana leaf. He pulled apart the hot wrapping, and *purrrrrrrrrr!* Away it flew to the nearest banana tree, where it landed, *ce!*

What's this! thought the hunter. I want to eat that bird, not chase it around! "Wife," he said, "bring me my bird at once!"

The poor woman went out to the grove of banana trees. There was the little bird, far out of reach, watching her carefully. She moved toward it slowly, trying to look friendly, and sang a little song.

The bird listened carefully, then fluttered off to another banana tree a little further away.

34

($\quad$ = 72)

The bird (CHORUS): Purrrrr ce!   Ja - ngu⌣o-nko - mbe   gwe   wa - nu - nga - mu!
Come   lick   me   clean   of   this   salt   you   used!

The wife followed the bird to its new tree. This time she sang more gently, coaxing it.

($\quad$ = 72)

SOLO: 'Ka - nyo - nyi   kaa - ba - ze,   'ka - nyo - nyi
Lit - tle   bird   hus - band   found,   lit - tle   bird

kaa - ba - ze   ne   bwo - ge - nda   sii - ku - lye.
hus - band   found,   don't   go,   I   won't   eat   you   up!

But the bird would not believe her. Off it flew to another tree further away.

($\quad$ = 72)

CH.:   Purrrrr ce!   Ja-ngu⌣o-nko - mbe   gwe   wa - nu - nga-mu!
Come lick   me   clean   of   this   salt   you   used!

35

She tried again in her very best voice.

And so it went, from one banana tree to the other down to the far end of the grove. She tried singing most politely; she tried singing most humbly; but the little bird would never let her get near.

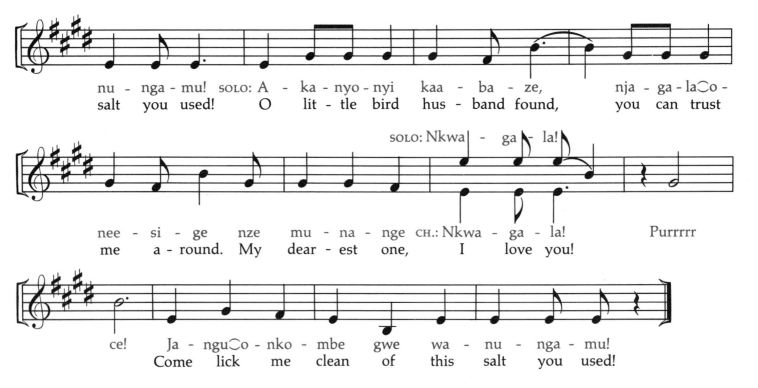

nu - nga - mu! SOLO: A - ka - nyo - nyi kaa - ba - ze, nja - ga - la⊃o -
salt you used! O lit - tle bird hus - band found, you can trust

SOLO: Nkwa - ga - la!

nee - si - ge nze mu - na - nge CH.: Nkwa - ga - la! Purrrrr
me a - round. My dear - est one, I love you!

ce! Ja - ngu⊃o - nko - mbe gwe wa - nu - nga - mu!
Come lick me clean of this salt you used!

When they came to the last tree in the banana grove, the little bird
flew off,

purr r r r r r r r r r r r r r r

and never was seen again.

38

So the wife came back to her husband without the bird, and her husband went back to his hunting without his lunch, and the little bird—well, it was a magic bird, of course!

And that is what I saw.

8. Awo!

The Baganda used to make their hoes out of forked sticks. To one fork they tied a forged iron blade. The other fork they used as a handle. The youngest girls in a work group would of course be given the poorest blades, and the singers of this song complain that, to make matters worse, they have been given blades tied to the wrong side of the fork so that the wood gave no support to the iron when it cut into the earth.

Form a line or a circle and jog in place, making gestures appropriate to the words you sing. When you try to walk (the final line of the chorus), act as if you have a crick in your back.

9. Nsangi

This is probably the best known story among the Baganda, and other peoples in Africa tell it, too. The teller mimes the action as his story unfolds, so after you and your audience have come to know this tale pretty well, you might try acting it out together.

Once upon a time there lived in Uganda a woman who had a beautiful daughter, Nsangi. They lived together in a lonely place. Their house was a cave, their door a large stone which they rolled across the entrance.

Every morning the mother left Nsangi alone while she went to take care of her grove of bananas, which was in a village some distance away. Nsangi would stay in the cave while she was gone and keep the entrance shut, for in those days gorillas wandered around the country looking for children to eat.

Before she left, the mother always sang a certain song to Nsangi. This is what she sang.

(♩. = 126)
Gently and smoothly

N - sa - ngi, Nsa - ngi, Nsa - ngi, N - sa - ngi mwa - na wa - nge,
my own ba - by,

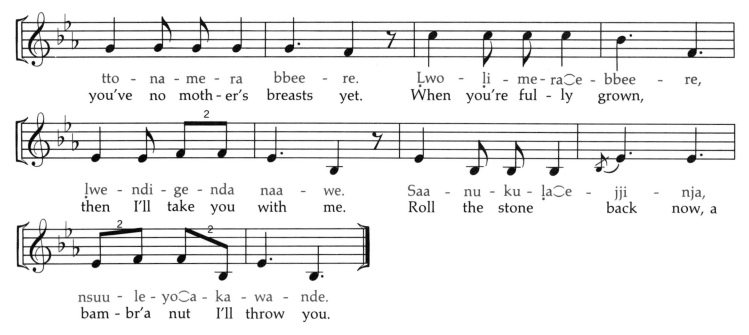

tto - na - me - ra bbee - re. Lwo - li - me - ra e - bbee - re,
you've no moth - er's breasts yet. When you're ful - ly grown,

lwe - ndi - ge - nda naa - we. Saa - nu - ku - la e - jji - nja,
then I'll take you with me. Roll the stone back now, a

nsuu - le - yo a - ka - wa - nde.
bam - br'a nut I'll throw you.

When her mother left the cave, Nsangi would roll the stone across the entrance to keep the gorillas out.

After working in the village most of the day, the mother would return with food she had prepared for them both to eat. She would stand outside the entrance and sing in her lovely voice:

($\downarrow$. = 126)

Gently and smoothly

N - sa - ngi, Nsa - ngi, Nsa - ngi, N - sa - ngi mwa - na wa - nge,
my own ba - by,

46

tto - na - me - ra bbee - re.
you've no moth - er's breasts yet.
Lwo - li - me - raᴐe - bbee - re Nsa-
When you're ful - ly grown, Nsangi,

ngi ndi - ge - nda naa - we.
then I'll take you with me.
Saa - nu - ku - laᴐe - jji - nja,
Roll the stone back now, a

nsuu - le - yoᴐa - ka - wa - nde.
bam - br'a nut I'll throw you.

Nsangi listened carefully. If she was sure it was her mother, she would roll back the stone.

Now it happened one morning that a gorilla was passing by as the mother sang her song to Nsangi. He hid behind a bush and listened. *Aha! That's what I'll do,* he thought. When the mother left, he went up to the mouth of the cave and sang her song in his deep, hoarse voice.

That did not sound at all like her mother! Nsangi did not dare to roll back the stone, so the gorilla had to go away without his meal.

He was back again, hiding behind the bush, when the mother returned from the village that afternoon. He listened carefully to her tone as she sang. When she went inside, he went off to practice.

The next morning he was there again, and the next afternoon, and

the day after that. Each time he listened carefully, and then went off to practice.

One afternoon Nsangi was sitting alone in the cave playing with some pebbles when the gorilla decided to try again. He stood outside the entrance, just where her mother usually stood, and he sang her mother's song, just the way her mother sang it.

Nsangi listened and listened, and it sounded so much like her mother that she rolled back the stone.

Whhhhhuppp! The gorilla grabbed her up and swallowed her in one gulp. Then he rolled the stone back in place and went away.

Not long after, the mother returned with fruits and cooked food for them to eat. She sang in her lovely voice, but there was no response. She rolled back the stone. *Ah!* There were the pebbles, and next to them the footprint of a gorilla.

Weeping and crying out for her lost child, the mother made her way to a certain witch-doctor who lived not far away. He consulted the spirits for her. "Nsangi will be found alive and well," he said, "inside the left little finger of one of the gorillas whom you will find standing beside a well in the forest."

He gave her powerful medicine to help her, and directions to the well, and ten strong men to go with her. Carrying stones and clubs, they went into the forest.

They found the well. Standing beside it in a line were the gorillas, just as the witch doctor had said. There were ten of them, and the mother saw that she had to question each of them in turn to find the guilty one.

She was frightened, but she went up to them and asked each one the same question, and each one answered her in the same way.

SOLO: GgweꞒo - li - dde Nsa - ngi! CHORUS: Aaa   baa - ba,   ssi - na - lya
You   ate   N - sa - ngi!   No,   dear - ie,   I've   not   eat'n

Nsa - ngi.   Nna - nyi - ni   bbu - toꞒe - ma - be - ga,   ya - li - dde   Nsa - ngi.
Nsa - ngi.   He   be - hind   me   with   the   tum - my,   he   ate   N - sa - ngi.

Bwe - nfu - ku - mu - laꞒe - ki - bu - to   nga   te - mu - li   Nsa - ngi.
If   I   emp - tied   out   my   stom - ach,   there'd   be   no   N - sa - ngi.

Be!   Fu - ku   fu - ku,   fu - ku!   Nga   te - mu - li   Nsa - ngi.
Look!   I'll   make   it   shake   and   shake!   See,   there's   no   N - sa - ngi.

When she came to the tenth gorilla, he trembled and hesitated and sang so badly they knew he must be the guilty one. When they cut off the little finger of his left hand, out sprang Nsangi! She ran to her mother and threw her arms around her.

The men chased away the guilty one with their stones and clubs, and brought the mother and child back to their home happy.

And that is what I saw.

10. Akanyonyi

When one of the Baganda falls sick and medicine fails to make him well, his family may consult someone who has the power to seek the advice of an oracle. It may turn out that some spirit or god is causing the trouble. The oracle will advise the family how to persuade it to leave them in peace. Often a goat, a cow, a hen, some beer, or a white cock is sacrificed.

Things offered to the gods have to be kept properly, and must not be eaten or sold. But just as naturally as lightning can strike and burn God's church, so a hen destined for sacrifice may be eaten by a wildcat. So this song about a black-eyed bird and some cow-peas is really saying, "God, don't think we have forgotten you. We give you offerings, and if they are not enough it is because some have been destroyed by unforeseen danger, so do not be angry."

The Baganda believe in a supreme Creator (Katonda). Lesser gods have responsibility for wars, for wealth, for mothers and babies, and so forth. "Zzaggulo" is the general name for a god, and so is "Lubaale." In the following song one could substitute the name of a particular spirit, for example the god of waters, "Mukasa" (musical rhythm ♫ | ♩), who has jurisdiction over storms, over all those who travel on lakes, and over Lake Victoria itself, the second largest lake in the world, which lies partly in the southeastern corner of Uganda.

nda naa - we!
go with you!

SOLO: A - ka-nyo-nyi⁀a - ka-ddu-ga-
A lit - tle bird a lit - tle

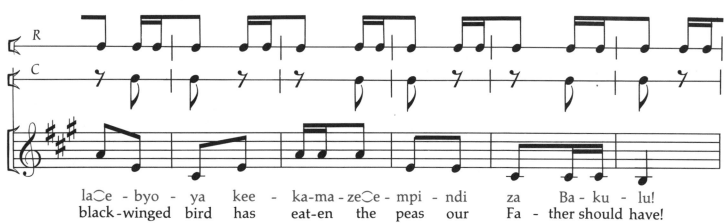

laᴐe - byo - ya   kee - ka-ma - zeᴐe - mpi - ndi   za   Ba - ku - lu!
black - winged   bird   has   eat-en   the   peas   our   Fa - ther should have!

we! Zza - ggu - lo   woo -   we! Zza - ggu - lo
you! Zza - ggu - lo,   Lord,   Lord! Zza - ggu - lo,

naa - ge - nda naa - we!
I shall   go with   you!

growing softer

11. Ttimba

The lizard of this story is as common in Uganda as the pigeon in our cities, or the birds above our meadows. Scurrying along with incredible speed, he can jump quite far and quite high if he has to. You will often see him pause for a moment and nod his head. Anything rougher than glass or smooth metal he climbs without difficulty, but he never starts up without seeming to give it a shake first, just to be sure.

ONCE UPON A TIME there lived in a certain village two good friends who liked nothing better than to sing and dance and play the drum.

Python was a fine dancer, Lizard was a wonderful singer, and both of them were very good drummers.

Now Lizard did not have a drum of his own. In those days drums were scarce, and very expensive. So he just went over to Python's house and borrowed *his* drum whenever he wanted to play.

Python's drum was called "The Drunkard." It was very beautiful, and he rarely let anyone but himself touch it. Except Lizard. He would let Lizard borrow it because they were such very good friends.

Now it happened that one day a messenger came to Lizard's house from the chief of a distant village. The chief knew of Lizard's wonderful singing, and he invited him to perform at his court.

To accompany his singing, Lizard needed a drum. He knew Python would never let "The Drunkard" out of the village. So he told his friend he wanted to practice at home for just three days, and Python, after he had carefully thought it over, agreed.

Then Python waited for the drum to be returned. One day. Two days. Three days. *Four days!*

Python went right over to Lizard's house. Lizard's wife was there, but she did not know of his trickery. So when Python asked where Lizard was, she told him. She also told him that Lizard would not return for a few more days.

Python was furious. *Oh, what a friend!* But there was nothing to do but return home and wait, which he did, muttering to himself about false friends and broken promises.

Lizard, meanwhile, was a smashing success at the chief's court. He drummed and sang for three days, and they asked him to stay four more, so he did. They gave him many gifts, and he was very pleased with himself. He decided that a really fine musician deserved a really fine drum, so when he went home he did not return "The Drunkard" to Python.

In fact, he ran out the back door of his house with the drum under his arm when Python came over. Python ran after him, but Lizard was the faster by far. He reached a tall, dead tree and climbed to the top of it with the drum.

When Python finally got there, Lizard looked down on his old friend and began to call him all the bad names he could think of.

"Hey, cripple! Hi, there, wiggle-belly! Want your drum, no-legs?" Python was not a good climber. Indeed, he could not climb at all. So he had to just sit there and take it. Lizard began to sing.

After a while, Python had had enough.

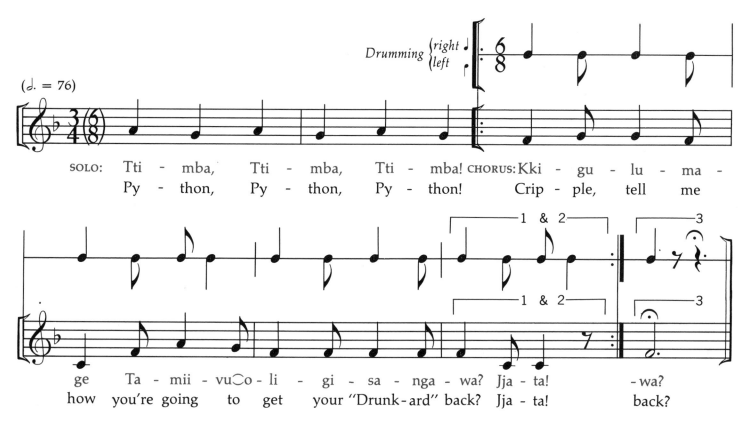

"No use sitting here listening to insults," he said, and went home.

Lizard sang on. Soon it was dark. By then he was tired of his song, so he climbed down the tree and went home himself.

There he got into a terrible fight with his wife. She thought it was just awful to keep his friend's drum, and gave him a real scolding. But Lizard would not return "The Drunkard."

He was up and away very early the next morning, taking the drum with him. When Python came by, Lizard's wife could not say where

63

he was. But Python heard the sound of a drum in the distance, so he went in that direction. Sure enough, there was Lizard up in a tree in the village playing on "The Drunkard."

"Hey, cripple! Come on up, wiggle-belly! No? So how'll you get your drum back, eh?" And Lizard began to sing.

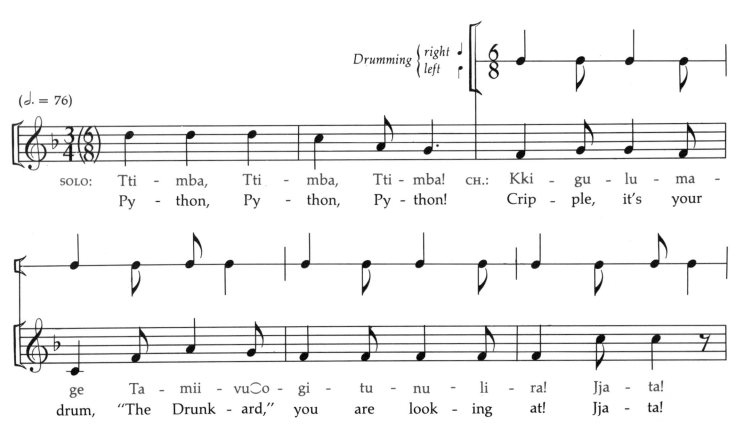

Kki - gu - lu - ma - ge Ta - mii - vu᷍o - li - gi - sa - nga -
Crip - ple, tell me how you're going to get your "Drunk - ard"

wa? Jja - ta! Kki - gu - lu - ma - ge Ta - mii - vu
back? Jja - ta! Crip - ple, look you now, "The Drunk - ard"

baa - gi - ku - jja - ko.
is no long - er yours.

That did it. Python was furious. He set about a plan to get back his drum.

He went to the Queen of the Safari Ants for help, but her soldiers were planning to invade a certain village the next day and she could not spare any.

He did not give up. He went to a nearby termite hill and spoke with Her Majesty the Queen. She agreed to help.

The next morning, just as he expected, Python heard his drum again. This time Lizard was up in a dead tree which stood by the edge of the river. Python wasted no time, but went immediately to the termite hill. The Queen ordered the attack.

Python went to the tree to watch Lizard dance and drum and sing at him from his perch up on a limb that hung out above the water. The termites went underground to the roots of the tree and began to eat them up.

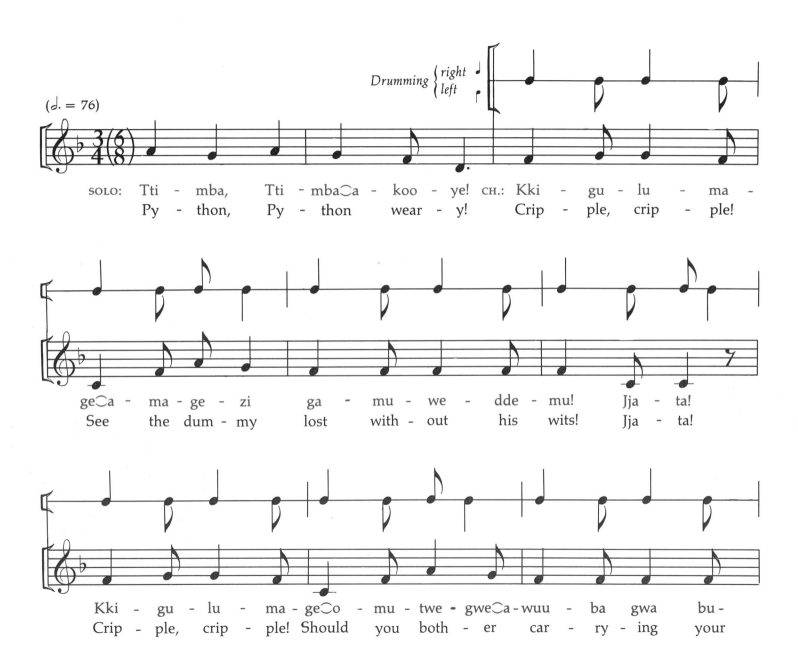

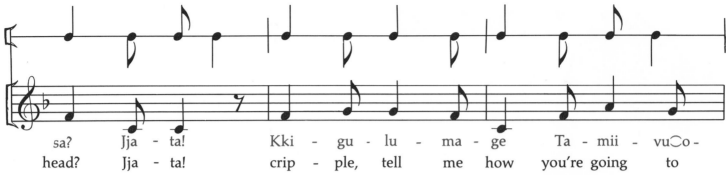

sa? Jja - ta! Kki - gu - lu - ma - ge Ta - mii - vu꞉o -
head? Jja - ta! crip - ple, tell me how you're going to

li - gi - sa - nga - wa?
get your "Drunk - ard" back?

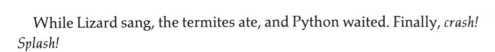

While Lizard sang, the termites ate, and Python waited. Finally, *crash!*
Splash!

68

The branch on which Lizard was dancing was the first to hit the water. In he went. He could not swim a stroke, so he began to drown.

"The Drunkard" landed within reach of Python. Python picked it up and put it aside in a safe place. Then, since he was a good swimmer, he went to the aid of his old friend. He carried a rope with him, and now he tied it around Lizard's neck. Then everyone on shore helped pull him in.

Lizard's life was saved, but the rope gave his neck an awful squeeze. His cheeks swelled up, and he was sick for many weeks.

His cheeks are still swollen, and now, before he climbs anything, he gives it a shake to see if the termites have been at it. He has never forgiven his wife for telling on him, and you can still see him stop from time to time to nod to himself, "A woman! A woman!"

And that is what I saw.

12. Woowooto

In the land of the Baganda, "Babirye" is the name taken by the elder girl of twins (the younger girl of twins will be named "Nakato," the elder boy of twins "Wasswa," and the younger boy of twins "Kato"). You may substitute any name you wish in place of "Babirye." Here is how to do it.

A name of three syllables with initial stress fits the same music as "Babirye." This includes English names we think of as having two syllables which end with a whispered consonant (the "k" of "Patrick," the "ce" of "Alice"). The Baganda add a vowel to these endings and let them sound.

Woo - woo - te - ra   Ba - bi - rye   ye - ba - ke.
                        Ti - mo - thy
                        Pa - tri - cka
                        A - li - ce
                        Ro - ber - ta   (the boy's name)

If the stress is on the second of three syllables, you do it this way.

Woo - woo - te - ra   Pa - tri - cia   ye - ba - ke.
                       Sa - man - tha
                       Ro - ber - ta   (the girl's name)

71

Names of two syllables, with the stress on the final syllable, are sung as follows.

Woo -woo - te - ra   Char - lene   ye - ba - ke.

Names of two syllables, with the stress on the first syllable go this way.

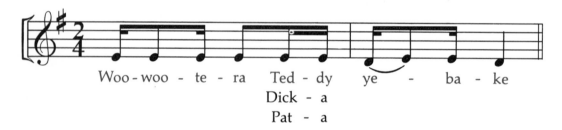

Woo - woo - te - ra   Ted - dy   ye - ba - ke
                      Dick - a
                      Pat - a

Names of one syllable have only one note, and are sung like this.

Woo - woo - te - ra   Tom   ye - ba - ke.
                      Bill
                      Jane

The Baganda will cut short a name, or otherwise squeeze it to fit
into the rhythm of the song. As in our own folk songs, the music does
not stop for the words.

SOLO: Woo - woo - to, woo - woo - to, CHORUS: woo - woo - te - ra⌒o - mwa - na ye - ba - ke.
Hush - a - bye, hush - a - bye,   lull   the   ba - by   to   sleep.

SOLO: Woo - woo - to, woo - woo - to, CH.: woo - woo - te - ra Ba - bi - rye ye - ba - ke.
Hush - a - bye, hush - a - bye,   lull   Ba - bi - rye   to   sleep.

SOLO: Woo - woo - to, woo - woo - to, CH.: sii - sii - ti - ra⌒o - mwa - na ye - ba - ke.
Hush - a - bye, hush - a - bye, rock   the   ba - by   to   sleep.

SOLO: Woo - woo - to, woo - woo - to, CH.: ffe - twa - ga - la 'mwa - na kwe - ba - ka.
Hush - a - bye, hush - a - bye, we want our ba - by   to   go   to   sleep.

SOLO: Woo - woo - to,   woo - woo - to, CH.: o - mwa - na   wa taa - ta   we - ba - ke.
Hush - a - bye,   hush - a - bye,   my dad - dy's ba - by   go   to sleep.

SOLO: Woo - woo - to,   woo - woo - to, CH.: o - mwa - na   wa maa - ma⌒o - mwa - ga - lwa.
Hush - a - bye,   hush - a - bye,   my ma - ma's ba - by   she loves   so   much.

SOLO: Woo - woo - to,   woo - woo - to, CH.: nku - yi - ti - re   ja - jja⌒a - kwe - ba - se.
Hush - a - bye,   hush - a - bye,   shall I   call grand - ma? She'll help   you sleep.

SOLO: Woo - woo - to,   woo - woo - to, CH.: o - mwo - yo   gwa maa - ma gu - lu - ma.
Hush - a - bye,   hush - a - bye,   your heart is   ach - ing   for your ma - ma.

SOLO: Woo - woo - to,   woo - woo - to, CH.: 'ku - fu - mbi - ra⌒a - ka - me - re   we - ba - ke.
Hush - a - bye,   hush - a - bye,   she's cook - ing food   for you, now   go   to sleep.

74

solo: Woo-woo-to, woo-woo-to, CH.: zi - bi - ri - za◡a - maa - so we - ba - ke.

Hush - a - bye, hush - a - bye, now close your eyes and sleep, ba - by, sleep.

solo: Woo-woo-to, woo-woo-to, CH.: sii - sii - ti - ra◡o-mwa - na we - ba - ke.

Hush - a - bye, hush - a - bye, rock the ba - by - to sleep.

solo: Woo-woo-to, woo-woo - to CH.: woo - woo - te - ra◡o-mwa - na ye - ba - ke.

Hush - a - bye, hush - a - bye, lull the ba - by to sleep.

solo: Woo-woo-to, woo - woo - to, CH.: woo - woo - te - ra◡o-mwa - na ye - ba - ke.

Hush - a - bye, hush - a - bye, lull the ba - by to sleep.

13. Ca, Ca, Ca

A mother will often rock her child, or toss it gently to the rhythm of this song. The refrain "Ca, ca, ca" (pronounced "cha, cha, cha") is an imitation of the sound of the metal anklets the mother often ties to her baby's feet when it first starts walking.

The song "Wavvuuvuumira" (No. 4 in this collection) is often added to the end of "Ca, Ca, Ca." You will find out how to do this in the introduction to No. 4.

You can clap on the first note of every measure.

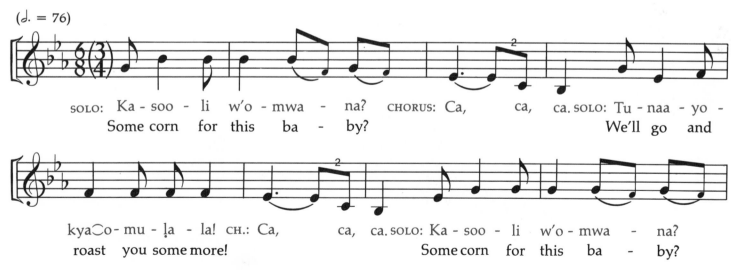

SOLO: Ka - soo - li w'o - mwa - na? CHORUS: Ca, ca, ca. SOLO: Tu - naa - yo -
Some corn for this ba - by? We'll go and

kya⌒o - mu - ḷa - la! CH.: Ca, ca, ca. SOLO: Ka - soo - li w'o - mwa - na?
roast you some more! Some corn for this ba - by?

CH.: Ca,   ca, ca. SOLO: Tu - naa - yo - kya◡o - mu - la̠ - la! CH.: Ca,   ca,
We'll   go   and   roast   you   some more!

ca. SOLO: Nku - yi - ti - re maa - ma? CH.: Ca,   ca, ca. SOLO: Ku - ba◡a - li
Then shall   I   call   ma - ma?   She's   in   the

mu - ni - mi - ro! CH.: Ca,   ca, ca. SOLO: Ka - nya - ma k'o - mwa - na?
gar - den work - ing!   Some meat   for   this   ba - by?

CH.: Ca,   ca, ca. SOLO: Tu - naa - yo - kya ka - la - la! CH.: Ca,   ca,
We'll   go   and   roast   you   some more!

(Growing softer to the end)

kyaⵎo - mu - ḷa - la! ᴄʜ.: Ca,   ca, ca. ꜱoʟo: Ka - soo - li   w'o - mwa   - na?
roast   you some more!   Some corn for   this   ba   - by?

ᴄʜ.: Ca,   ca, ca. ꜱoʟo: Tu - naa - yo - kyaⵎo - mu - ḷa - la! ᴄʜ.: Ca,   ca,
We'll go   and roast   you some more!

ca. ꜱoʟo: Bi - nyee - bwa by'o-mwa - na?   ᴄʜ.: Ca,   ca, ca. ꜱoʟo: Tu - naa - yo -
Pea - nuts for this ba   - by?   We'll go and

kyaⵎe - bi - ra - la! ᴄʜ.: Ca,   ca, ca.
roast   you some more!

ABOUT THE AUTHOR   William Moses Serwadda has been singing, dancing, and drumming since he was five years old. The son of a Mukunja farmer from the shores of Lake Victoria, he is presently on the faculty of the Department of Music and Dance at Makerere University in Kampala, Uganda. For years he ran a biweekly television program of traditional music for children there, and is a member of the Nyonza Singers, generally rated the finest such group in the country. His personal musical style is considered by the Ministry of Culture to be a model for the performance of traditional music, and since Uganda's independence in 1962 he has been asked many times to go around the country training local clubs dedicated to traditional music. He holds a Master's Degree in African Dance from the Institute of African Studies at the University of Ghana, and has directed choirs in many festivals of African music in his own country, Europe, the United States, and Canada. The songs and stories in this book are from his own large collection of folk material, much of it acquired as a child in the household of his grandfather, an administrator in the Bukunja area appointed by the King of the Baganda.

ABOUT THE EDITOR   Hewitt Pantaleoni trained as a musicologist at Harvard and then turned to ethnomusicology, and in particular to the study of African music. He received his Ph.D. in World Music from Wesleyan University (Connecticut) and presently teaches Western, non-Western, and folk music at the State University College at Oneonta, New York. He has taught American children to sing the songs in this book in the original African language, and finds that the stories go best when you learn to do them by heart in a lively way that encourages the children to join in the singing.